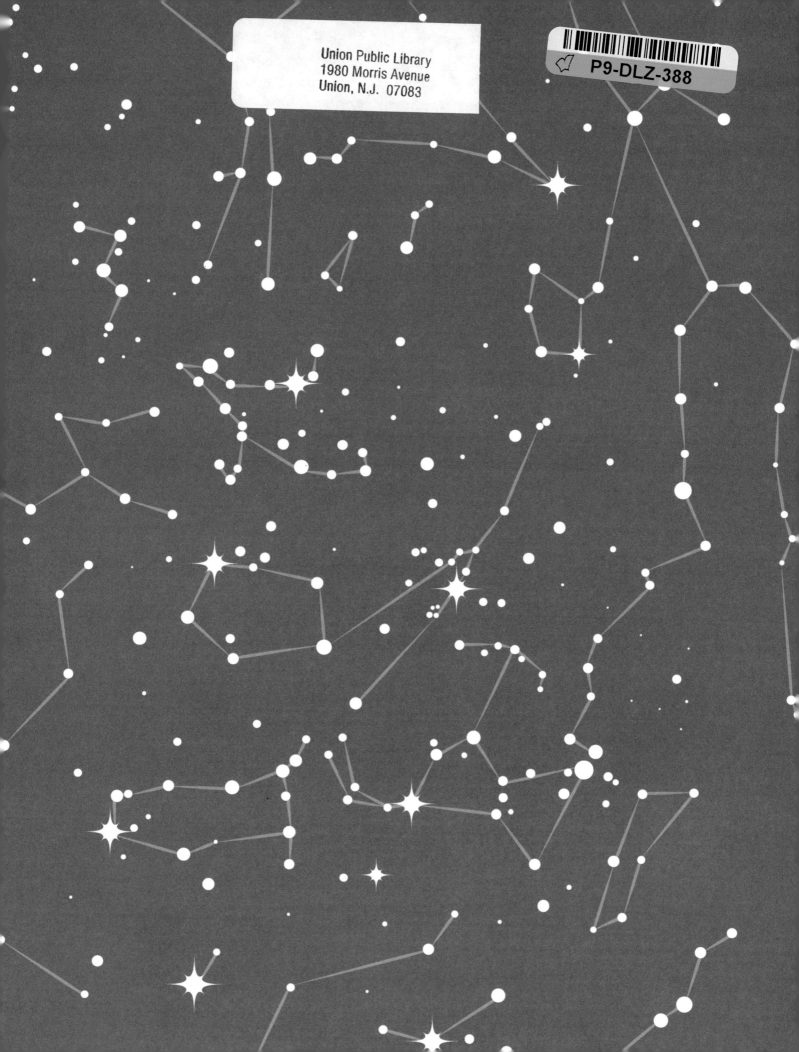

Annie Jump Cannon, ASTRONOMER

Annie Jump Cannon, ASTRONOMER

By Carole Gerber
Illustrated by Christina Wald

PELICAN PUBLISHING COMPANY
Gretna 2011

Copyright © 2011
By Carole Gerber

Illustrations copyright © 2011
By Christina Wald

The word "Pelican" and the depiction of a pelican are trademarks of Pelican Publishing Company, Inc., and are registered in the U.S. Patent and Trademark Office.

Library of Congress Cataloging-in-Publication Data

Gerber, Carole.
  Annie Jump Cannon, astronomer / by Carole Gerber ; illustrated by Christina Wald.
    p. cm.
  ISBN 978-1-58980-911-6 (hardcover : alk. paper) 1. Cannon, Annie Jump, 1863-1941—Juvenile literature. 2. Women astronomers—United States—Biography—Juvenile literature. 3. Astronomers—United States—Biography—Juvenile literature. I. Wald, Christina, ill. II. Title.
  QB36.C34G47 2011
  520.92—dc23
  [B]

                                                2011012147

Printed in Singapore
Published by Pelican Publishing Company, Inc.
1000 Burmaster Street, Gretna, Louisiana 70053

On clear nights, they climbed, up, up, up the long staircase of their three-story home. Annie, holding a flickering candle, led the way. Following behind was her mother, Mary Elizabeth, carrying charts from her school days.

When they reached the attic, they opened the trapdoor and stepped onto the roof. By candlelight, they matched the charts of the heavens to the stars overhead. In this way, Annie learned the names of constellations visible from her rooftop in Dover, Delaware.

Annie's father worried about the candle starting a fire. But he did not forbid stargazing. Instead, Wilson Cannon allowed his daughter to develop her quick mind.

Annie Jump Cannon was born on December 11, 1863, during the Civil War. She was given her mother's maiden name as a middle name.

Annie was a lively child who liked to play the piano. She grew up secure and happy. Her father's company built ships and the family lived in a nineteen-room house. When a nearby boys' school began admitting girls, Annie's parents enrolled her.

In 1880, she graduated first in her class and gave an uplifting valedictorian speech. She titled it "Golden Grains from Life's Harvest Field." Like her classmates, she was eager to get on with her life. However, she didn't yet know what lay ahead.

But her father did. While on a trip, he had toured Wellesley College in Massachusetts. He was impressed that a women's college offered the same courses as male universities.

That fall, Annie's parents enrolled her in the only women's college offering physics classes. One of the first teachers Annie met at Wellesley was Sarah Frances Whiting. All students were required to take her physics classes, where they learned about the science of energy and matter.

The women conducted lab experiments that helped them discover scientific principles. This type of learning suited Annie. She liked figuring things out for herself.

Annie loved Wellesley! Her grades were outstanding. However, during her sophomore year, she had a setback that would have defeated a less determined girl.

After being sick with scarlet fever, Annie developed an ear infection that left her partially deaf. Still, she vowed to graduate with her class, and she did! In 1884, Annie earned a degree in physics.

$N^2\left(\frac{\partial^4 z}{\partial x^4} + \frac{\partial^4 z}{\partial x^2 \partial y^2} + \frac{\partial^4 z}{\partial y^4}\right) + \frac{\partial^2 z}{\partial t^2} = 0$
N^2 IS Co
β
α

Upon graduation, at her mother's urging, she moved home. Because her family was wealthy, Annie did not need to find a job. Instead, she taught herself photography. This skill came in handy in 1892 when she traveled to Europe with a friend to photograph an eclipse of the sun.

Córdova Mosque 1892

Solar Eclipse 1892

When Annie returned, the Blair Camera Company printed a booklet of her photographs. Titled *In the Footsteps of Columbus,* it was sold at the 1893 Chicago World's Fair. Annie was excited to see her name on the cover.

Afterwards, though, she felt restless. Annie and her mother were extremely close and enjoyed their time together. However, Annie was thirty years old and wanted a more independent life.

In December of 1893, Annie's mother died unexpectedly. Annie was grief-stricken but took comfort from recalling how she and her mother had studied the stars. In 1894, she returned to Wellesley to study astronomy. She worked as Sarah Whiting's teaching assistant to support herself.

Annie—who had been so bored at home—was again cheerful and busy. She enjoyed her classes at Wellesley. She also took classes at nearby Radcliffe, the women's college at Harvard. There, she used the telescope at Harvard Observatory. This decision set the course for Annie's career.

In 1896, the director of the observatory hired Annie. Edward Pickering needed her help with a project: photographing and classifying all the stars in the sky. The widow of an amateur astronomer named Henry Draper paid for the project.

Annie soon learned she would not be taking pictures of the stars. Instead, like Pickering's other female assistants, Annie would examine the photographs taken by male astronomers. The women would determine each star's position in the sky and the type of light it emitted.

No one had ever before undertaken such a massive project! Compiling the nine volumes of the *Henry Draper Catalogue* became Annie's life's work.

Harvard Observatory

The astronomers attached a device called a spectograph to their telescopes. It separated each star's light into different wavelengths. Annie had used a similar device in her physics classes.

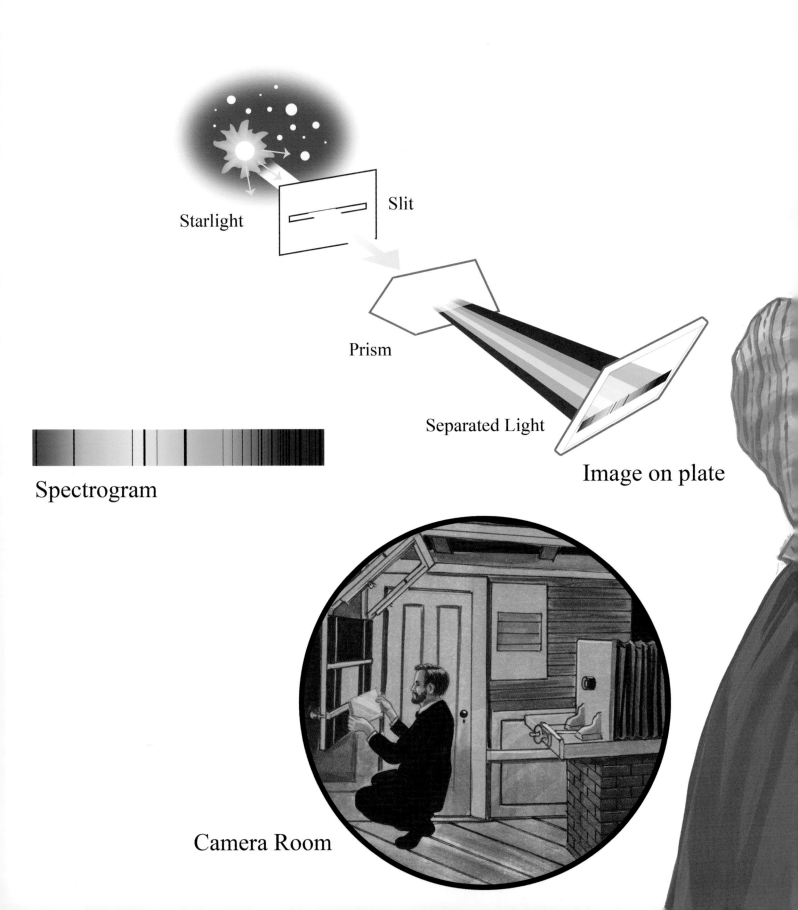

Starlight

Slit

Prism

Separated Light

Image on plate

Spectrogram

Camera Room

The images of each star's light, or spectrum, were then imprinted onto photographic glass plates called spectrograms. The assistants who examined the plates were known as "computers." Their job was to analyze the type of light coming from each star by looking for telltale dark lines. These lines helped them determine what the star was made of and how hot it was. For their work, the women were paid one-fourth of men's wages.

Why weren't Pickering's assistants allowed to photograph the stars? Mr. Pickering had three reasons. He felt women should not work at night with men. He believed women were better at detailed tasks. And, perhaps most importantly, he could pay women far less than men.

"These women are capable of doing as much good routine work as astronomers who would receive much larger salaries," he explained. "Three or four times as many assistants can thus be employed."

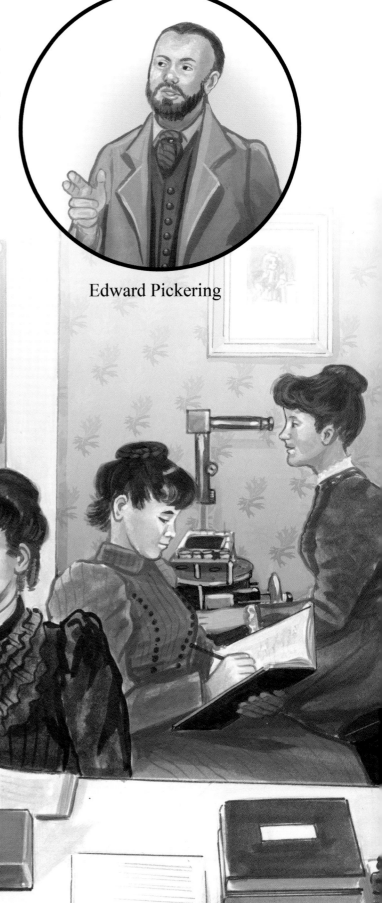

Edward Pickering

The computers used magnifying glasses to examine the spectographs. They called out facts about each star's light to other women called "recorders." The recorders wrote the facts into notebooks. Annie had sharp eyes and a good memory. She did not hear sounds that distracted others. She became the fastest computer and could classify three stars a minute!

However, she saw a problem with the A to O alphabetical system that was used to classify the stars' spectra. Annie noticed that the brightest O stars were the hottest. The A stars were the third hottest. This led her, between 1911 and 1915, to develop a shorter and more accurate system for classifying stars that is still used.

Annie ranked stars from the hottest—white and blue in color—to the cooler red ones. She put the hottest stars in the O category. The next hottest were in the B category, and so on. The coolest were classified as M stars.

The letters in Annie's "hottest to coolest system" were OBAFGKM. Annie came up with a sentence that made the system easy to remember:

Oh

Be

A

Fine

Girl

Kiss

Me

While working, Annie continued her studies. In 1907, at age forty-four, she earned a master's degree in astronomy. She did not take time off to celebrate. Instead, she continued speeding through spectrograms. Between 1911 and 1915, she classified nearly 250,000 stars!

In 1922, Annie was sent to Harvard's observatory in Peru for a special assignment. Finally, she was permitted to use a spectrograph and telescope as the male astronomers did. When she returned to Massachusetts, she classified and catalogued the thousands of southern hemisphere stars she had photographed.

Annie became known as "the census-taker of the stars" and earned many awards. The one she valued most came in 1925. Oxford University honored her at age sixty-two with a doctor of science degree. She was the first woman to receive it.

When she was seventy-five, Harvard finally gave Annie the title professor of astronomy.

As a child, Annie became fascinated by stars. This fascination lasted a lifetime, ending with her death at age seventy-seven.

Shortly before she died on April 13, 1941, Annie wrote to a friend: *"At the Observatory, I am classifying, classifying. . . . Of course, I love to do it."*

Annie's love for her work shaped her life and led her to set a world record that still stands. Annie Jump Cannon classified the spectra of more than 400,000 stars!

Timeline

1863: Annie Jump Cannon is born in Dover, Delaware, on December 11.

1874: Enrolls at the Wilmington Conference Academy.

1880: Graduates first in her class in June.

1880: Enters Wellesley College in Wellesley, Massachusetts.

1884: Graduates from Wellesley with a degree in physics.

1892: Travels to Europe and uses a Blair camera to photograph her trip. The Blair Camera Company prints a book about her travels and sells it at the 1893 Chicago World's Fair.

1894: Returns to Wellesley to work as a teaching assistant and enrolls at Radcliffe College to study astronomy.

1896: Hired by the Harvard Observatory to classify and compile stars for *The Henry Draper Catalogue.*

1907: Earns a master's degree in astronomy from Radcliffe College.

1911: Promoted to curator of astronomical photography at Harvard Observatory.

1911-1915: Develops a simplified system to classify stars' light. Her Harvard Spectral Classification System is still used.

1922: Sent to Harvard's observatory in Peru to photograph and classify southern hemisphere stars.

1924: Moves into "Star Cottage," across from Harvard Observatory, and lives there for the rest of her life.

1925: Travels to England to receive a doctor of science degree from Oxford University.

1929: Named by the National League of Women Voters as one of the "twelve greatest living American women."

1931: Receives the Henry Draper Medal from the National Academy of Sciences.

1934: Establishes the Annie J. Cannon Prize, which each year recognizes outstanding women astronomers.

1938: Promoted to professor of astronomy by Harvard.

1941: Dies on April 13 at age seventy-seven in Cambridge.

Selected Bibliography

"Annie Jump Cannon." *School and Society* 53, no. 1373 (April 19, 1941): 507.

"Annie Jump Cannon House." Web site of Wesley College, President's Residence. http://www.wesley.edu/index.cfm?fuseaction=administration.cannonhouse.

Bok, Priscilla F. "Annie Jump Cannon, 1863-1941." Publications of the Astronomical Society of the Pacific (1941): 168-70.

Driscoll, Sally. "Annie Jump Cannon: Background." Retrieved from MasterFILE Premier Database, 2006.

Emberlin, Diane. *Contributions of Women in Science.* Minneapolis: Dillon Press, 1977.

Hennessey, Logan. "Annie Jump Cannon (1863-1941)." Web site of Wellesley College, Women in Science. http://www.wellesley.edu/astronomy/annie/.

"Henry Draper Catalogue (HD)." *Encyclopædia Britannica Online.* http://www.britannica.com/EBchecked/topic/262045/Henry-Draper-Catalogue.

Kohlmiller, Paul. "The Most Important Woman Astronomer." *San Jose Astronomical Association Ephemeris* 17, no. 12 (December 2006): 3.

Rossiter, Margaret W. *Women Scientists in America, Vol. 1: Struggles and Strategies to 1940.* Baltimore: The Johns Hopkins University Press, 1982.

Welther, Barbara. *Annie and the Stars of Many Colors: A Portrait of Astronomer Annie Jump Cannon.* Directed by Alex Griswold. Harvard-Smithsonian Center for Astrophysics, 1993.